بسم الله الرحمن الرحيم

The Preservation of Ḥadīth

In the name of Allah; the Most Gracious, the Most Merciful.

All praise is due to Allah; Lord of all the worlds; and peace and blessings be upon the most Honorable of Messengers, Muḥammad, and upon his family and companions, and all those who follow them in righteousness, until the Day of Judgment.

Truly, my prayer and my service of sacrifice, my life and my death, are all for Allah, the Cherisher of the Worlds...

The PRESERVATION *of* ḤADĪTH

Ibrahim Madani

MADANIA PUBLICATIONS

First Edition June 2010

Translation: Asim Ahmad
Production Manager: Hassan Shibly
Editing: Mayada Osman & Qudsia Ahmad
Book Design: Jennifer Benaggoun
Arabic Calligraphy: Mohammad Alagha
Cover Design: MK & ZH
Cover Photo: Mas'ud Ahmad Khan

Library of Congress: 2010930478
ISBN: 978-1-936157-02-0

Distributed in USA by Al-Rashad Books
sales@al-rashad.com
1·330·388·4103

Distributed in Canada by Al Zahra Booksellers
info@alzahraonline.com
1·416·312·7213

Distributed in UK by Azhar Academy Ltd. London
sales@azharacademy.com
+44·208·911·9797

Published by
Madania Publications
New York USA ☙ 1·716·480·0163
www.madaniapublications.com ❧ *info@madaniapublications.com*

محمد رسول الله

مَنْ يُطِعِ الرَّسُولَ فَقَدْ أَطَاعَ اللَّهَ

Whosoever follows the Blessed Prophet ﷺ has followed Allah سبحانه وتعالى.

وَمَا آتَاكُمُ الرَّسُولُ فَخُذُوهُ وَمَا نَهَاكُمْ عَنْهُ فَانْتَهُوا

Whatever the Prophet ﷺ gives you, accept it; and whatever he disapproves of, abstain from it.

TRANSLITERATION KEY

ء (إ أ)	' (the *hamza* is produced by a sudden stop in the airstream similar to the sound in the middle of the exclamation, *uh-oh*.)	ك	*k*
ا	*a, ā*	ل	*l*
ب	*b*	م	*m*
ت	*t*	ن	*n*
ث	*th* (is pronounced like the *th* in *thick* and *thumb*)	و	*w*
ج	*j*	ه	*h*
ح	*ḥ* (a heavy *h* sound produced in the center of the throat)	ي	*y, ī, i*
خ	kh (a guttural *k* sound produced in the upper throat and sounding similar to the *ch* in German as in *Bach*.)		
د	*d*		
ذ	*dh* (is pronounced like the *th* in *though* and *thus*)		
ر	*r*		
ز	*z*		
س	*s*		
ش	*sh*		
ص	*ṣ* (an emphatic *s*)		
ض	*ḍ* (an emphatic *d*)		
ط	*ṭ* (an emphatic *t*)		
ظ	*ẓ* (an emphatic *dh*)		
ع	', *'a, 'i, 'u* (produced in the center of the throat)		
غ	*gh* (a guttural *g* sound produced in the upper throat)		
ف	*f*		
ق	*q* (a heavy *k* sound)		

رضي الله عنها	*Raḍiya Allahu 'anhā* – may Allah ﷻ be pleased with her (used following mention of a female companion of the Blessed Prophet ﷺ)
رضي الله عنه	*Raḍiya Allahu 'anhu* – may Allah ﷻ be pleased with him (used following mention of a male companion of the Blessed Prophet ﷺ)
رضي الله عنهم	*Raḍiya Allahu 'anhum* – may Allah ﷻ be pleased with them (used following mention of a group of companions of the Blessed Prophet ﷺ)
ﷺ	*Ṣallallahu 'alaihi wa Sallam* – may the peace and blessings be upon him (used following mention of the Blessed Prophet ﷺ)
ﷻ	*Jalla Jallāluhū* – Exalted is His majesty (used following mention of Allah ﷻ)
عليه السلام	*'alaihi al-Salām* - may peace be upon him (used following mention of prophets)

TABLE OF CONTENTS

Introduction xi

Introduction to the Study of Ḥadīth 1

Preservation of Ḥadīth 1

Two Types of Revelation: The Spoken and the Unspoken 3

Upholding the Meaning of the Qur'an 7

The Methodologies of Preservation of Ḥadīth 7

The Sharp Memory of Ibn Rāhwai 10

The Sharp Memory of Abū Zur'a 11

Waḥshī's رضي الله عنه Memory 13

Love For Knowledge 14

The Principle of Practice 17

Documentation 18

The Collection of Abū Huraira رضي الله عنه 20

The Book of Anas رضي الله عنه 21

The Different Types of Ḥadīth Books 22

The Saḥīḥ and Ḍa'īf Ḥadīth 24

Branches of Aḥadīth According to the Chain 26

The Definition of a Saḥīḥ Ḥadīth 26
Do Bukhārī and Muslim Contain All the Authentic Aḥadīth? 29
Is A Ḥadīth Given Preference Because it is in Bukhārī or Muslim? 30
The Six Books of Ḥadīth and the Objectives of the Imams 31
Brief Biographies of the Great Ḥadīth Masters 34

INTRODUCTION

It is not possible in this day and age to comprehend the great sacrifices that were made by the hadith masters [*muḥaddithīn*] or the difficulties and barriers they struggled to overcome for the preservation of hadith. It is a result of these sacrifices that today each word, in fact each letter of the aḥādīth are fully preserved. The rules the hadith masters established to preserve the hadith and by which this branch of knowledge became a distinct science are necessary for one to learn and make headway into both the knowledge of hadith and principles of hadith [*uṣūl al-ḥadīth*].

This short booklet is written to introduce the reader to the knowledge of hadith. It discusses important issues such as how the hadith were compiled, the preservation of hadith, principles regarding the authenticity and weakness in a hadith, the importance of hadith and the various types of hadith books. It ends with short biographies of some of the famous hadith masters. This booklet may be looked upon as a first step in acquiring the insight that is necessary for advancing in this science. After reading this booklet, if one feels a renewed connection with the hadith, it is hoped that it will be a way of salvation for its author. The readers are requested to pray for the author, his parents and his family and that Allah bless them in this world and the Hereafter.

Ibrahim Madani
June 2010

INTRODUCTION TO THE STUDY OF ḤADĪTH

The way our love for our parents is understood by realization of the sacrifices they made for us, likewise our realization of how ḥadīth were preserved, their authority in Islam, and the work and sacrifices of the ḥadīth masters in the science of ḥadīth, helps increase our love and adoration for our predecessors. In addition, we will appreciate the true value of ḥadīth and be more scrupulous before judging a hadith as weak.

PRESERVATION OF ḤADĪTH

Allah ﷾ states in the Qur'an:

لَقَدْ مَنَّ اللَّهُ عَلَى الْمُؤْمِنِينَ إِذْ بَعَثَ فِيهِمْ رَسُولًا مِنْ أَنْفُسِهِمْ يَتْلُو عَلَيْهِمْ آيَاتِهِ
وَيُزَكِّيهِمْ وَيُعَلِّمُهُمُ الْكِتَابَ وَالْحِكْمَةَ وَإِنْ كَانُوا مِنْ قَبْلُ لَفِي ضَلَالٍ مُبِينٍ

Indeed Allah ﷾ has already done a favor to the believers, when He raised amongst them a messenger from themselves to recite to them His verses, purify them and teach them the book and the wisdom.[1]

This aya explains one of the most important responsibilities of the beloved Blessed Prophet ﷺ: to teach the Book. This responsibility consists of not just teaching the pronunciation and reading of

[1] 3:164

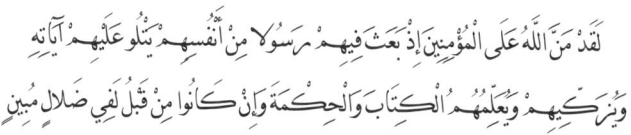

the Book [as that is already covered in the first responsibility, i.e. '*to recite to them His verses*'], but more importantly, the meaning of the Qur'an. It would be meaningless for a Muslim to try to understand the meaning and message of the Qur'an without the Blessed Prophet ﷺ as a teacher to explain it to us.

Proficiency in the Arabic language alone cannot help us grasp the meaning of the Qur'an. Remember, the Ṣaḥāba ﷺ, who spoke fluent Arabic, always turned to the Blessed Prophet ﷺ to understand the deeper meanings of the Qur'an. The Qur'an's words and its meanings were explained both verbally and practically by the Blessed Prophet ﷺ. These sayings and explanations of the Blessed Prophet ﷺ are called ḥādīth and provide us with the the most authentic commentary of the Qur'an. Therefore, Allah's ﷻ promise to preserve the Qur'an meant preservation of the aḥādīth as well.

However the preservation of words alone serves little purpose. For example, if the Qur'an commands Muslims to establish ṣalāt, but we are unable to understand what this command entails [such as how to perform it], then what benefit is there in preserving the words "establish the ṣalāt?" This proves that the preservation of the Qur'an, by necessity, includes preservation of the ḥādīth. Without ḥādīth, the īmān of a Muslim is incomplete. After all, how do we know that the Qur'an is the book of Allah ﷻ?

If we know the Qur'an and its place, it is only because the Blessed Prophet ﷺ said, "This is the Qur'an; it is the word of Allah ﷻ." If we were to reject this ḥadīth of the Blessed Prophet ﷺ then the whole foundation of Islam collapses. We would not know that the Qur'an is what it claims to be.

Allah ﷻ says to the Blessed Prophet ﷺ in the Qur'an:

وَأَنزَلْنَا إِلَيْكَ الذِّكْرَ لِتُبَيِّنَ لِلنَّاسِ مَا نُزِّلَ إِلَيْهِمْ وَلَعَلَّهُمْ يَتَفَكَّرُونَ

And We have sent unto you the message, that you may explain clearly to men what is sent for them, and that they may give thought.[2]

This aya proves that the fundamental role of ḥādīth is to reveal the meaning of the Qur'an, which means that the Qur'an cannot be understood without the aḥādīth.

TWO TYPES OF REVELATION: THE SPOKEN AND THE UNSPOKEN

The Blessed Prophet ﷺ received two types of divine revelations. One is the spoken [*matluww*] and the second, the unspoken [*ghair-matluww*]. The spoken revelation is that which is recited [i.e., the Qur'an]; the unspoken revelation is that which is not recited [i.e., the aḥādīth of the Blessed Prophet ﷺ]. An indication of the roots of the unspoken revelation can be found in the ayas of the Qur'an. Allah ﷻ says in the Holy Qur'an:

وَمَا جَعَلْنَا الْقِبْلَةَ الَّتِي كُنتَ عَلَيْهَا إِلَّا لِنَعْلَمَ مَن يَتَّبِعُ الرَّسُولَ مِمَّن يَنقَلِبُ عَلَىٰ عَقِبَيْهِ

And We appointed the qibla to which you were used only to test those who followed the Messenger from those who would turn on their heels.[3]

To gain a broader understanding of this aya, it is important that we look into its historical background.

---

[2] 16:44

[3] 2:143

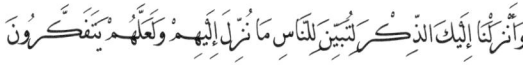

Shortly after the migration to Madina, the Blessed Prophet ﷺ and the Ṣaḥāba ؓ were told to pray towards Masjid al-Aqṣā in Jerusalem. Masjid al-Aqṣā became the *qibla* of the Muslims for seventeen months. After seventeen months, the order to pray towards Masjid al-Aqṣā was abrogated and Muslims were ordered to pray towards Makka. This order was established through the following aya:

فَوَلِّ وَجْهَكَ شَطْرَ الْمَسْجِدِ الْحَرَامِ

Turn your faces towards al-Masjid al-Ḥarām.[4]

This order broke the sanctimonious silence of the hypocrites. They criticized the changing of the qibla and argued, "Why did the Qur'an need to make 'amends' regarding the direction of prayer for the Muslims?" The above aya explains that the purpose behind the change of the qibla was to test the īmān of the Muslims and see whether they would obey or disobey the Blessed Prophet ﷺ. Read this aya carefully once again:

وَمَا جَعَلْنَا الْقِبْلَةَ الَّتِي كُنتَ عَلَيْهَا إِلَّا لِنَعْلَمَ مَن يَتَّبِعُ الرَّسُولَ مِمَّن يَنقَلِبُ عَلَىٰ عَقِبَيْهِ

And ***We appointed the qibla*** *to which you were used only to test those who followed the messenger from those who would turn on their heels.*[5]

In this aya, Allah ﷻ mentions the first order, which was to face towards Jerusalem, as His own order. This impresses upon the reader the fact that Allah ﷻ himself was behind the order to face Masjid

[4] 2:143

[5] Ibid

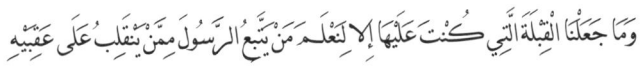

al-Aqṣā. But when we read the Qur'an we do not find any such aya in which Allah ﷻ ordered the Muslims to pray towards Jerusalem.

The fact is that this order came from the Blessed Prophet ﷺ and not from any aya of the Qur'an. The aya does NOT say, "*The Blessed Prophet ﷺ enacted the order…*" rather it says, "*We appointed the qibla….*" This brings us to the understanding that the order of the Blessed Prophet ﷺ is no different from the order of Allah ﷻ.

The proof is so self-evident it does not require any further clarification. This clear statement from the Qur'an regarding the order given by the Blessed Prophet ﷺ demonstrates a fundamental belief about the aḥādīth of the Blessed Prophet ﷺ: that they are a form of revelation. And this is what is known as the unspoken or unrecited revelation.

The aya mentioned above also reveals some other important points:

1. A special type of revelation was sent to the Blessed Prophet ﷺ which was not a part of the Qur'an.
2. These revelations were from Allah ﷻ.
3. Similarly, the rulings that derived from the unspoken revelations were also the rulings of Allah ﷻ.

All the Ṣaḥāba ؓ were obligated to fulfill the orders of the unspoken revelations in the same manner as they were the spoken revelation [Qur'an]. Some orders were revealed to test the īmān of the Muslims, particularly those orders that were revealed through the unspoken revelation, to see whether they obeyed the orders. Many other examples could be cited, but they have not been mentioned for the sake of brevity.

While this aforementioned proof highlights the importance of the aḥādīth and their validity as an authority in Islam, it also establishes that the preservation of the Qur'an includes preservation of the ḥādīth. The Qur'an itself is the essence of Islamic thought and is the final word in this matter. The Qur'an states:

مَنْ يُطِعِ الرَّسُولَ فَقَدْ أَطَاعَ اللَّهَ

Whosoever follows the Blessed Prophet ﷺ has followed Allah ‹.[6]

In this aya the Qur'an orders us to adhere to the way of the Blessed Prophet ﷺ, as adherence to the Blessed Prophet ﷺ is adherence to Allah ﷻ. Once, a woman came to the famous Ṣaḥābī ؓ, 'Abd Allāh ibn Mas'ūd ؓ. She said, "I have heard you stop people from doing certain things even though I have read the Qur'an from cover to cover and I have never read the Qur'an ordering us to abstain from these things." 'Abd Allāh ibn Mas'ūd ؓ replied, "Had you read the Qur'an you would have found it. Have you not read this aya of the Qur'an:

وَمَا آتَاكُمُ الرَّسُولُ فَخُذُوهُ وَمَا نَهَاكُمْ عَنْهُ فَانْتَهُوا

Whatever the Prophet ﷺ gives you, accept it; and whatever he disapproves of, abstain from it.[7]

From this incident we learn that this aya incorporates the aḥādīth of the Blessed Prophet ﷺ and establishes the authority of the aḥādīth in Islam.

---

[6] 4:80

[7] 59:7

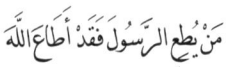

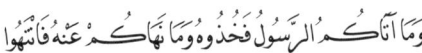

UPHOLDING THE MEANING OF THE QUR'AN

If Allah ﷻ himself has taken the responsibility to preserve ḥādīth, as indeed He has, then who can question their validity and authority? A closer look at the unique methods by which the aḥādīth have been preserved reveal them to be simply awe-inspiring and a miracle in their own right. These methods are briefly outlined below.

THE METHODOLOGIES OF PRESERVATION OF HADĪTH

Generally, three methods were used to preserved ḥādīth:

The first method was memorization. The Arabs were renowned for their memories, particularly their ability to memorize long poems along with the biographies of their authors. They could recollect long lists of the names of poets' forefathers and their lineages. Not only that, the Arabs also memorized the lineage of their horses, even the horse's gaits. Thus, thousands of names were at the tip of their tongues, and through the blessings of the aḥādīth Allah ﷻ added to their proficiency in the art of memorization.

This simple method of preserving ḥadīth cannot be ignored, especially when eminent personalities like Imam Bukhārī have recorded incidents such as that of Marwān, which illustrate the extraordinary memory of the Arabs. Marwān was the first governor of Damascus and also the first emir of the Umayyad Dynasty.

His secretary, Abū al-Zaʿza, narrates that once Marwān called the eminent Ṣaḥābī ؓ, Abū Huraira ؓ, to his court. It is said that the reason behind this rare invitation of a Ṣaḥābī ؓ to Marwān's court was that Marwān doubted the large number of aḥādīth Abū

Huraira had memorized and frequently narrated. Before Abū Huraira entered, Marwan instructed his secretary, Abū al-Za'za, to hide behind a curtain with a pen and paper in his hand. He said, "I am going to ask him to narrate some aḥādīth; while he narrates, I want you to pen all the aḥādīth down."

When Abū Huraira entered, Marwān asked him about some aḥādīth. As Abū Huraira began narrating, Abū al-Za'za wrote them down. Abū al-Za'za says, "Abū Huraira continued narrating for a long time and I saw that I had written a large collection of aḥādīth on my papers."

It seems from Abū al-Za'za's words "ḥadīthun kathīrun" that he had indeed recorded a large collection of aḥādīth on his paper.

Meanwhile, Abū Huraira had no idea he was being tested. After this, Abū Huraira left. Marwān preserved the scrolls of the secretly recorded ḥādīth and waited for the following year. A year later, Marwān again invited Abū Huraira to honor him with his presence. Once again, Marwan told Abū al-Za'za to hide behind the curtain with the papers on which he had written the aḥādīth the previous year. He said, "I am going to repeat the same questions I asked last year. Check and see if it coincides with the aḥādīth of the previous year."

It was an extemporaneous test for Abū Huraira. Abū al-Za'za says, "So Marwān kept the year old aḥādīth in his hands. After one year, he again called upon Abū Huraira as I sat quietly behind the curtain. As he put the questions, I looked into my papers. He did not add to or subtract from even one word of a ḥadīth."[8]

Though it is not possible to ascertain the exact number of aḥādīth noted, it is clear that it was a significant number. A

[8] Kitāb al-Kunā, pg. 33

similar incident occurred with Ibn Shihāb al-Zuhrī during the same time period. Hishām ibn 'Abd al-Malik called Ibn Shihāb to his court. In this incident, it is clearly mentioned that Ibn Shihāb narrated exactly four hundred aḥādīth.

It is also mentioned in the books of history that Hishām tested Ibn Zuhrī's memory as Marwān had Abū Huraira's ﷺ. The story goes like this:

> One day, Ibn Shihāb came to the court for something. Hishām personally requested Ibn Shihāb to write some aḥādīth for his son, the prince. Ibn Shihāb accepted; a scribe was called in and the dictation began. Dhahabī writes, "Ibn Shihāb dictated four hundred aḥādīth to the prince."
>
> Then Ibn Shihāb left. When Ibn Shihāb returned a month later, Hishām feigned remorse by saying to Ibn Shihāb, "I am saddened to tell you that the parchments on which the aḥādīth were written have disappeared and they are nowhere to be found."
>
> "What is this to cry about?" asked Ibn Shihāb. "Call the scribe and I will dictate them again."
>
> This was precisely the objective of Hishām. He quickly ordered the scribe to his court. Ibn Shihāb dictated the same aḥādīth over again. The first collection of aḥādīth had not really disappeared, it was only a ploy to test Ibn Shihāb's memory of aḥādīth. When Ibn Shihāb left the court, Hisham compared the older copy with the new one and saw that no change had been made to the original copy of aḥādīth.[9]

Had it not been for the *ḥuffāẓ* [memorizers] of Qura'n today, the claim "not one addition had been made to the original copy of aḥādīth" would seem like a tale from a children's storybook. Today one can test a *ḥāfiẓ* [memorizer] from the Qura'n, which

[9] Tadhkirat al-Ḥuffāẓ 1/110

is bigger than a collection of four hundred aḥādīth. Having him read a chapter of the Qur'an and then asking him to recite it from memory will prove that word for word, there will be no difference between the first recitation and the second. One is thus forced to admit that neither any addition nor any subtraction was made to these aḥādīth.

THE SHARP MEMORY OF IBN RĀHWAI

The story of Ibn Rāhwai, the teacher of Imam Bukhārī, and his gift of memory is a story that has stuck to his name. The story about the memory of Ibn Rāhwai is widely narrated in scholarly circles. Once he was discussing some juridical issues with another scholar in the private chambers of 'Abd Allāh ibn Ṭāhir. They disagreed on the text of a certain book. Ibn Rāhwai asked 'Abd Allāh ibn Ṭāhir to have the book checked out from his library. The book was brought before the two scholars. Ibn Asākir writes in *The History of Damascus* that after this disagreement, Ibn Rāhwai said to 'Abd Allāh ibn Ṭāhir, "Open to the eleventh page of the book, on the seventh line you will find what I have been saying."

'Abd Allāh ibn Ṭāhir flipped to the eleventh page and found it exactly as Ibn Rāhwai had quoted. At this point, 'Abd Allāh ibn Ṭāhir rose to the occasion and said to Ibn Rāhwai, "I knew you had a lot of Shari'a rulings put to memory, but this unprecedented revelation of your sharp memory has indeed left me wonderstruck."[10]

This incident leaves no doubt about the sharpness of Ibn Rāhwai's memory, but is it not true that we find ḥuffāẓ in almost every area, city and village who recite ayas of the Qur'an and can instantly

[10] Ibid 8/137

locate its place in the Qur'an? The reality is that Ibn Rāhwai is not the only example amongst the scholars who memorized aḥādīth of the Blessed Prophet ﷺ.

THE SHARP MEMORY OF ABŪ ZUR'A

Ḥāfiẓ Abū Zur'a was a famous imam and a distinguished scholar in the science of the biographies of narrators [*asmā' al-rijjāl*]. Ibn Abī Ḥātim has narrated this story about him:

> Once Ibn Warā, whose name was Muḥammud ibn Muslim, and Faḍl ibn 'Abbās, whose nickname was Faḍluk al-Ṣāigh, came to Ḥāfiẓ Abū Zur'a. Both of them began to argue about some Shari'a ruling. Ibn Wāra quoted a ḥadīth to support his position, but Faḍluk rejected the ḥadīth and insisted that it was not the correct wording of the ḥadīth. Ibn Wāra asked, "Then what are the proper words of this ḥadīth?"
>
> Faḍluk quoted the ḥadīth in the way he thought was correct. As the debate continued, Abū Zur'a quietly listened. Ibn Wāra then turned to Abū Zur'a and asked, "What are the actual words of the ḥadīth?"
>
> Abū Zur'a avoided answering, but when Ibn Wāra insisted Abū Zur'a said, "Go call my nephew, Abū al-Qāsim."
>
> When Abū al-Qāsim arrived, Ḥāfiẓ Abū Zur'a said to him, "Go to the library, leave the first, second and third shelf. In the shelf after, you will find a volume of books. Do not pick any other except the seventeenth volume and bring it to me."
>
> Abū al-Qāsim went and returned with the book. Ḥāfiẓ Abū Zur'a flipped through the pages until he reached the page on which the ḥadīth was written. He handed the open book over to Ibn Wāra. Ibn Wāra read through the ḥadīth and then acknowledged his mistake.

After this incident, we should contemplate the claim of Abū Zur'a, which has been narrated by Ibn Ḥajar with reference from Abū Ja'far Tastarī in his book *al-Tahẓīb.* Abū Zur'a claimed, "Fifty years have passed since I have written aḥādīth, and all the books are in my house. From the time I wrote them, I have never read those aḥādīth, but I know which ḥadīth is in what book, on what page and on what line."[11]

Similarly, Imam Sha'bī says, "I have never put pen to paper [i.e. never wrote aḥādīth] and never did I have to request a narrator to repeat a ḥādīth because I have forgotten it."[12]

Ḥāshid ibn Ismā'īl was a classmate of Imam Bukhārī. He himself was an eyewitness to the following incident. He narrates:

> Imam Bukhari was still a young boy when he came to our class to learn aḥādīth with us. Generally, students noted down the aḥādīth of the teacher as he narrated them. However, we would notice Imam Bukhārī sitting quietly, listening to the teacher without writing anything down. For some days we observed this with silence, but when he continued to behave in this manner, we started to chide him for wasting time in the class and not writing anything down. Imam Bukhārī ignored these objections and did not rebut them.
>
> One day, people lectured him too much, and he became angry. He said, "What are you trying to say? Go bring your notes, sit here around me and I will, by memory, say everything you have written."
>
> Ḥāshid finally admits, "He recited over fifteen thousand aḥādīth from memory."[13]

---

[11] al-Tahẓīb, 7/30

[12] Ibn Sa'ad, 6/249

[13] Tadhkirat al-Ḥuffāẓ, 2/556

There are numerous incidents of this kind, so many in fact that it would take perhaps another book to attempt to narrate them all. These few incidents which have been mentioned; however, should suffice to gauge the extraordinary memories of these scholars.

WAḤSHĪ'S ※ MEMORY

Ja'far ibn 'Amr al-Ḍumarī ※ says:

> 'Ubaid Allāh ibn 'Adī ibn Khiyār and I went to Ḥimṣ [Syria]. At that time, Waḥshī ※ was also settled in Ḥimṣ; therefore we went to go and meet him. As soon as he saw 'Ubaid Allāh, he asked, "Are you the son of 'Adī ibn Khiyār?"
>
> 'Ubaid Allāh replied, "Yes, I am his son. But how do you know me, I have never met you before."
>
> Waḥshī ※ replied, "It is true we have never met before, but when you were born I picked you up and gave you to the mid-wife. When I picked you up, everything was covered except your feet. Today, when you came I saw your feet and recognized you."

Waḥshī saw 'Ubaid Allah ibn 'Adi ibn Khiyār after how many years? Ḥāfiẓ ibn Ḥajar writes in Fatḥ al-Bārī, "After birth, he saw him for the second time after fifty years".[14] And the amazing part is that Waḥshī recognized him immediately.[15]

The books of history and the books on the biographies of the narrators are full of such incidents. Firstly Allah ※ blessed them with extraordinary memories, and, secondly, they were so passionate about aḥādīth that they took every step and made every effort within their means to gain knowledge of it. Their endeavors and hardships in this regard are not difficult for us to realize and understand in our times.

[14] Fatḥ al-Bārī, *Qauluhū Qatl Ḥamza ibn 'Abd al-Muṭṭalib*

[15] al-Iṣāba, 7/441

LOVE FOR KNOWLEDGE

These scholars possessed a type of motivation that is almost beyond belief. Indeed, their efforts to preserve aḥādīth were like odysseys that were full of hardships and tribulations that are inconceivable today.

Abū Huraira ﷺ once said:

> You people think that Abū Huraira ﷺ narrates too many aḥādīth from the Blessed Prophet ﷺ, but I swear by Allah ﷻ that I was a poor man who stayed with the Blessed Prophet ﷺ night and day while the *Muhājirīn* [emigrants] did business in the markets and the *Anṣār* [helpers] were busy cultivating their fields.[16]

On another occasion he explained how he spent his time with the Blessed Prophet ﷺ:

> I came to the Blessed Prophet ﷺ at Khaibar. I was then over thirty years old and stayed with the Blessed Prophet ﷺ until he died. I was always by his side; I was with him when he went to meet his wives. I always helped him and stayed with him during his journeys on haj and in the path of Allah ﷻ.

Thus, he relished those "student years" of his life. He would say:

> I swear by Allah ﷻ that sometimes I would be starving. I would hold my stomach, lean on the ground and tie stones to it."[17] Sometimes I felt dizzy and would fall between 'Āisha's ﷺ home and the pulpit of the Blessed Prophet ﷺ. People thought I had become insane, but what do I have to do with insanity? It was from hunger.[18]

'Abd Allāh ibn 'Abbās ﷺ also narrates the story of his "student days."

[16] Bukhārī, *mā Jā' fi al-Gharas*

[17] Ibid 7/435

[18] Bukhārī, *mā Dhakar al-Nabiyy wa Ḥadḍa*

He said:

> I had thirst for the knowledge of aḥādīth. Whenever I found out someone had heard something from the Blessed Prophet ﷺ about some matter, I went to his house. If I found that he was taking a nap in the afternoon, I lay down at the threshold of the door, wrapped my shawl into a roll and used it as a pillow. The wind would blow sand into my face as I lay waiting. I would bear this condition until the person came to the door.
>
> When he saw me there he would say, "What brings you here, O nephew of the Blessed Prophet ﷺ?"
>
> I would reply that, "I have heard you narrate a certain ḥādīth of the Blessed Prophet ﷺ. I just want to hear that ḥadīth."
>
> The Ṣaḥābī ؓ would say, "You could have sent somebody or I would have come myself."
>
> I would say, "I am obligated to come to your house.'[19]

Abū Ayyūb Anṣārī ؓ also heard thousands of aḥādīth from the Blessed Prophet ﷺ. Once, he was unsure of a particular ḥadīth which he himself had heard from the Blessed Prophet ﷺ. At the time of hearing this ḥadīth another Ṣaḥābī ؓ, 'Uqba ibn 'Āmir ؓ was also present. Although 'Uqba ؓ had settled in Egypt by this time, Abū Ayyūb Anṣārī ؓ traveled to Egypt to verify one ḥadīth. After arriving at Uqba's ؓ house, Abū Ayyūb Anṣārī ؓ said, "Narrate the ḥadīth to me which you heard from the Blessed Prophet ﷺ about finding faults in other Muslim brethren. Now none is left except you and I who have heard this ḥadīth from the Blessed Prophet ﷺ." 'Uqba ؓ narrated the ḥadīth to Abū Ayyūb Anṣārī ؓ. The actual ḥadīth says:

من ستر مؤمنا في الدنيا على عورة ستره الله يوم القيامة

[19] Sunan al-Dārimī, *al-Riḥla fī Ṭalab al-'Ilm*

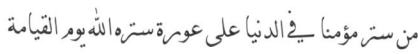

Allah ﷻ will cover the fault in the Hereafter of one who covers the fault of his Muslim brother.[20]

What happened after he heard this ḥadīth is even more astonishing. Abū Ayyūb Anṣārī ؓ listened to the ḥadīth, saddled his horse, mounted it and immediately set back for Madina. He did not even open his baggage in Egypt.[21]

Obviously if so much effort was made for a single ḥadīth, one can only imagine the dedication and perseverance that was called for in order to preserve all the aḥādīth. These words have been repeated by 'Ubaida, the ḥadīth master, who used to say, "We should learn the aḥādīth of the Blessed Prophet ﷺ the way we memorize the Qur'an."[22]

Abū 'Alī al-Naishābūrī said the following about the famous memorizer of ḥadīth [*ḥāfiẓ al-ḥadīth*] Ibn Khuzaima, "Ibn Khuzaima memorized the aḥādīth of Shari'a rulings like recitors [*qurrā'*] memorize the Qur'an."[23]

Imam Dhahabī quoted in the biography of Isrā'īl ibn Yūnus that he used to say, "I used to memorize the aḥādīth narrated by my grandfather, Abū Isḥāq, as I would memorize the suras of Qur'an."[24]

It is mentioned in the biography of Ismā'īl ibn Rajā', "He used to gather the children who studied in centers for memorization of Qur'an and recited aḥādīth to them so he would not forget the aḥādīth."[25]

---

[20] Musnad Aḥmad, 28/658|Muṣannaf 'Abd al-Razzāq, *Satr al-Muslim*

[21] Jāmi'u Bayān al-'Ilm, pg.94

[22] Tārīkh Damishq, 8/436

[23] Tadhkirat al-Ḥuffāẓ 2/723

[24] Tadhkirat al-Ḥuffāẓ 199

[25] Jāmi'u Bayān al-'Ilm, pg.102

Similarly, the Ṣaḥāba ؓ also stressed this point upon their students by saying, "The Blessed Prophet ﷺ narrated the ḥadīth to us and we memorized it; therefore, you should also memorize the aḥādīth as we did."[26]

Once 'Alī ؓ was advising his students, "Always repeat the aḥādīth over and over again. If you do not, then your knowledge will diminish."[27]

'Abd Allāh ibn Mas'ūd ؓ also advised his students when he said, "Repeat the aḥādīth regularly because this is the way to keep them alive."[28]

THE PRINCIPLE OF PRACTICE

The second method of preservation is called the "principle of practice." This is the most powerful system of preservation of aḥādīth, and it is both unprecedented and unrivaled in the annals of history. A non-Muslim could never even imagine how the practices of the Ṣaḥāba ؓ nurtured each and every Sunna of the Blessed Prophet ﷺ. In fact, even most of the Muslims of today cannot understand the love of the Ṣaḥāba ؓ for the Blessed Prophet ﷺ, their adherence to his personal habits or the unique relationship between them and the Blessed Prophet ﷺ. Never in history has mankind seen an example as great as the Ṣaḥāba ؓ.

'Urwa ibn Masūd Thaqafī ؓ had not yet embraced Islam. In the treaty of Ḥudaibiya he closely observed the Ṣaḥāba ؓ and finally said:

> Oh people! I have visited the courts of kings on many occasions. I have come face to face with the emperor of Rome, the king of

---

[26] Ibid, pg. 64

[27] Ibid, pg. 101

[28] Ma'rifat 'Ulūm al-Ḥadīth, pg. 141

> Persia and Negus of Abyssinia, but by Allah ﷻ I have not seen a people revere their king the way I saw the Companions ؓ of Muḥammad ﷺ revere him. By Allah ﷻ, if he as much as spits, it is rubbed on the hands, face and body of one of the Companions ؓ before it hits the ground. He does not order but they run to fulfill it. He performs ablution and the Companions ؓ compete with each other to take the dripping water. When he talks, they quell their voices. They cannot look at him fully out of awe for him.[29]

Anas ؓ relates, "I saw the Blessed Prophet ﷺ searching for pieces of squash in a bowl of curry. From that day on, I loved squash."[30]

Anas ؓ was a Ṣaḥābī ؓ of the Blessed Prophet ﷺ; his love for the Blessed Prophet ﷺ compelled him to also love squash. If he did not love squash after knowing that the Blessed Prophet ﷺ liked it, then some difference would remain between the Ṣaḥābī ؓ and the Blessed Prophet ﷺ. But there was no question for the Companions ؓ, of their own likes or dislikes once a Sunna was established in any matter.

Because of their deep love for the Blessed Prophet ﷺ, the Ṣaḥāba ؓ preserved every aspect of the Blessed Prophet's ﷺ life; his worship, the way he ate, slept, worked, etc. In the time of the Ṣaḥāba ؓ, there was no other way of doing anything except the way of the Sunna. Thousands of such examples of the devotion of the Ṣaḥāba ؓ for the Sunna of the Blessed Prophet ﷺ are narrated in aḥādīth. In fact, all aḥādīth are a manifestation of the love of the Ṣaḥāba ؓ for the Blessed Prophet ﷺ.

DOCUMENTATION

The third method of preservation is the written documentation of the aḥādīth. Some people believe that aḥādīth were first documented

---

[29] Bukhārī, *al-Shurūt fi al-Jihād*

[30] Bukhārī, *al-Sahūla wa al-Samāḥa fi al-Sharā'*

in the third century, while other more reliable scholars hold the view that documentation of aḥādīth began in the first century. If we go deeper into this matter, we will find that that the aḥādīth were even written during the time of the Blessed Prophet ﷺ and his Ṣaḥāba ؓ.

The difference between the recording of aḥādīth in the time of the Blessed Prophet ﷺ and those written after he passed away was that not everyone was allowed to note down the aḥādīth in his lifetime. The ones who were allowed wrote the aḥādīth with the permission of the Blessed Prophet ﷺ himself. However, during the end of his life, the Blessed Prophet ﷺ abrogated this restriction and gave permission for everyone to write his aḥādīth. He said, "Write! There is no harm."[31] Once he said, "Preserve knowledge by writing it."[32]

'Abd Allāh ibn 'Amr ibn al-'Āṣ ؓ said that the Blessed Prophet ﷺ told him, "Preserve the knowledge."

He replied, "How should I preserve it?"

He said, "By writing it."[33]

This is why many collections of aḥādīth were compiled during the lifetime of the Blessed Prophet ﷺ. For example, there is the *al-Ṣaḥīfat al-Ṣādiqa* [*The Authentic Scroll*] in which 'Abd Allāh ibn 'Amr ibn al-'Āṣ ؓ wrote all the aḥādīth of the Blessed Prophet ﷺ. He himself said:

> I wrote whatever I heard from the Blessed Prophet ﷺ and memorized it. Some members of Quraish discouraged me from recording the aḥādīth. They said, "Do you write whatever you hear from the Prophet? He is a man; sometimes he jokes and sometimes he gets angry like any other person."

[31] Tadrīb al-Rāwī, pg.286

[32] Jāmi'a Bayān al-'Ilm, pg.72

[33] Mustadrak Ḥākim, 1/106

What they meant was that the Blessed Prophet ﷺ may get angry or joke and say what he did not mean to say, therefore one should not write down everything he says. 'Abd Allāh ibn 'Amr ibn al-'Āṣ ؓ brought this to the Blessed Prophet's ﷺ attention. The Blessed Prophet ﷺ pointed to his lips and said, "I swear in the name of Allah ﷻ, in whose hands is my life, that nothing but truth [*ḥaqq*] comes from these two lips."[34]

This was clear proof that every word of the Blessed Prophet ﷺ was the truth and that all of it should be put to paper. To fulfill this order, 'Abd Allāh ibn 'Amr ibn al-'Āṣ ؓ compiled a large selection of aḥādīth into a book which he appropriately titled *al-Ṣaḥīfat al-Ṣādiqa*.

THE COLLECTION OF ABŪ HURAIRA ؓ

It is known that Abū Huraira ؓ recorded the largest collection of aḥādīth, which was also documented. Imam Ibn 'Abd al-Barr narrates on the authority of Ḥasan ibn 'Amr, who says:

> I narrated a ḥadīth to Abū Huraira ؓ but he rejected it. I said, "I have heard this ḥadīth from you."
>
> He said, "If you have heard this ḥadīth from me, then I must have it written down." He held my hand and took me to his room. He showed me his library of books that comprised of his narrations from the Blessed Prophet ﷺ. He found the ḥadīth I had narrated in the books. After that, Abū Huraira ؓ said to me, "Did I not tell you that if I narrated any ḥadīth to you I must have it written down?"[35]

Ḥāfiẓ ibn Ḥajar has also narrated this ḥadīth in his book, *Fatḥ al-Bārī*, with another chain. This incident proves that Abū Huraira

[34] Abū Dāwūd, *fī Kitābat al-'Ilm*

[35] Mustadrak Ḥākim, 3/584

ﷺ did not document only a few aḥādīth, but in fact all the aḥādīth which eventually became his store of ḥadīth books.

However this method of preservation does not stop here. Even his students wrote the aḥādīth they heard from him. One student named Bashīr ibn Nuḥaiq wrote:

> I wrote down whatever aḥādīth I heard from Abū Huraira ؓ. When I decided to leave, I read all the aḥādīth he narrated to me by his side. Then I asked, "Are these all the aḥādīth you narrated to me?"

> He replied, "Yes."[36]

THE BOOK OF ANAS ؓ

Anas ؓ also wrote down his collection of aḥādīth. Saʿīd ibn Hilāl says in the *Mustadrak* of Ḥākim:

> When we asked a lot of questions, Anas ؓ pulled out a big bag, opened it and would say, "These are the aḥādīth that I have heard from the Blessed Prophet ﷺ. I wrote them down and have already shown them to the Blessed Prophet ﷺ."[37]

The summary of this introduction is that Allah ﷻ created certain tools, like the photographic memories of the Arabs, to help preserve the aḥādīth. He then gave this knowledge a practical shape through the lives of the Ṣaḥāba ؓ to protect it from becoming another philosophy. This preservation came by way of the principle of practice. Then He produced the scholars and their students, who dedicated their lives to documenting these aḥādīth. Then a time came when hundreds of scholars compiled all of the aḥādīth and put them in book form. We will discuss this last stage in the later sections of this book.

---

[36] Muṣṣanaf Ibn Abī Shaiba, *Man Rakhkhaṣa fī Kitāb al-ʿIlm*

[37] Mustadrak Ḥākim, 3/664

THE DIFFERENT TYPES OF ḤADĪTH BOOKS

Many different types of books have been written on the subject of aḥādīth. The ḥadīth masters have categorized the different types of books on aḥādīth. Below, we will mention some of them:

al-Jawāmi': *al-Jawāmi'* is the plural of *Jāmi'*. Jāmi' denotes the ḥadīth book which includes eight different subjects: (1) Biographies, (2) Morals, (3) Beliefs, (4) Degeneration [*Fitan*], (5) Signs of the Day of Judgment, (6) Rulings of the Shari'a, (7) Virtues of the Ṣaḥāba ﷺ [and others] and (8) Exegesis of the Qur'an.

The first Jāmi' ever written was called *Jāmi' Mu'ammar ibn Rāshid*. Mu'ammar ibn Rashid was a close student of Imam Zuhrī. This book came out in the first century and is now unavailable. The second Jāmi' was written by Sufyān al-Thaurī; his book is also unavailable. The third Jāmi' was titled *Jāmi' 'Abd al-Razzāq*, though it is better known by the name *Muṣannaf 'Abd al-Razzāq*. Then, of course, the other well-known Jāmi' are *Bukhārī* and *Muslim*.

Interestingly, some ḥadīth masters have a difference of opinion about *Muslim*. Many say it is amongst the Jāmi', while others say it is not, as its section on the exegesis of the Qur'an is too short to be labeled a Jāmi'.

al-Sunan: These are ḥadīth books in which the aḥādīth are arranged in the order upon which the chapters of the books of *fiqh* [Islamic jurisprudence] are arranged. This type of book was first called *al-Abwāb* [chapters] but was later changed to *al-Sunan*. *Sunan al-Nisā'ī*, *Sunan Abū Dāwud*, *Sunan al-Tirmidhī* and *Sunan Ibn Māja* all belong in this category.

al-Masānīd: *Masanīd* is the plural of *Musnad*. The aḥādīth in these books are arranged in the order of the names of the Ṣaḥāba ﵃. The arrangement of these aḥādīth can be on many different levels. For example, they can be arranged in the order of the greatest of the Ṣaḥāba ﵃ downwards or in alphabetical order of the names of the Ṣaḥāba ﵃.

al-Mu'jam: This is a book of ḥadīth in which the aḥādīth are arranged in order of the names of the teachers from whom the author narrated his ḥadīth.

Al-Mustadrak: The books of ḥadīth that have been compiled according to the conditions [for accepting a ḥadīth into a ḥadīth book] laid down in another ḥadīth book. However, it does not include the ḥadīth being narrated in the original ḥadīth book. The *Mustadrak* of Ḥākim, for example, compiles aḥādīth that fulfill the conditions Imam Bukhārī laid for accepting a ḥadīth in his book.

al-Mustakhraj: This compilation takes aḥādīth of another book and narrates the different chains of transmission for every ḥadīth that differs from the chain of transmission mentioned in that ḥadīth book. Though the chains of transmission of one ḥadīth contain different narrators, they eventually ascend to the same person.

al-'Ilal: A book of ḥadīth that reveals the various faults found in the chain of transmission of a ḥadīth.

al-Arba'īn: A compilation of forty aḥādīth.

al-Ta'ālīq: The book of aḥadīth that narrates aḥādīth without mention of the chain of transmission, such as *al-Mishkāt al-Maṣābīḥ*.

Sharḥ al-Āthār: A book of ḥadīth that narrates apparently conflicting aḥādīth and offers an explanation that eliminates the contradiction. If the contradiction between the aḥādīth cannot be removed, then it provides the proofs and reasons for giving preference to one ḥadīth over another.

al-Jam'a: The ḥadīth book that abridges a collection of aḥādīth from different books and eliminates repetition of aḥādīth.

al-Adhkār: The book of ḥadīth that compiles the ḥadīth that narrate different *du'ās* [supplications] and forms of *dhikr* [uttered devotions].

al-Mauḍū'āt: The book of ḥadīth that collects fabricated aḥādīth that are scattered in various ḥadīth books.

There are many other types of ḥadīth books which are not being mentioned here, both for the sake of brevity and because understanding the various other types of compilations requires an expertise in the field of ḥadīth.

THE SAḤĪḤ AND ḌA'ĪF ḤADĪTH

In many books of aḥādīth, we read the words authentic [*ṣaḥīḥ*] and weak [*ḍa'īf*]. Many people understand authentic to be the opposite of weak, and when this word does not appear after a ḥadīth, they misinterpret it as weak. This is a common mistake because the words authentic and weak are actually nomenclatures of the ḥadīth masters. Over fifty terms are used by the ḥadīth masters [to define a ḥadīth], authentic being only one of them. When a ḥadīth is not identified as authentic, it may fall under the category of any of the other forty-nine types of ḥadīth and may not necessarily be weak.

Many times, a ḥadīth is authentic, but the ḥadīth masters reject it while another ḥadīth may be weak but the ḥadīth masters say it is okay to act upon. There are many reasons behind this. For example, it is possible that the authentic ḥadīth is abrogated and the weak ḥadīth supported by the practice of the Ṣaḥāba ﷺ.

Below, we will briefly examine some of these different types of ḥādīth:

Marfū': Any ḥadīth that is attributed to the Blessed Prophet ﷺ. Such a ḥadīth is identified by the words of the narrator when he says, "the Blessed Prophet ﷺ said," "the Blessed Prophet ﷺ did this," "the Blessed Prophet ﷺ remained quiet on this occasion," "when such and such thing was said," or that "this ḥadīth is attributed to the Blessed Prophet ﷺ" or that "Ibn 'Abbās ؓ attributed this ḥadīth to the Blessed Prophet ﷺ." Thus, any ḥadīth attributed to the Blessed Prophet ﷺ is a *marfū'* ḥadīth.

Mauqūf: A narration attributed to a Ṣaḥābī ؓ. A *mauqūf* narration is recognized by the words of the narrator when he says, "Ibn 'Abbās ؓ said" or "Ibn 'Abbās ؓ did such and such thing" or "it is said that this ḥadīth is narrated as *mauqūf*."

Maqtū': Any narration that is attributed to the first successors of the Ṣaḥāba ؓ [*tābi'īn*]. Some ḥadīth masters also call a *maqtū'* narration *athar* [trace]. The term athar makes it easy to distinguish ḥadīth of the Blessed Prophet ﷺ from the narrations of the Ṣaḥāba ؓ and the first successors. Thus ḥadīth of the Blessed Prophet ﷺ are known as ḥadīth, while the narrations of the Ṣaḥāba ؓ and the first successors are called *āthār* [plural of athar], though the word athar is frequently used for the aḥādīth of the Blessed Prophet ﷺ also.

BRANCHES OF ḤADĪTH ACCORDING TO THE CHAIN

Muttaṣil: This defines a ḥadīth in which the chain of narrators is complete and no missing link is found between the narrators.

Munqaṭi': A ḥadīth in which one or more than one narrator is missing from a chain of narrators [regardless of whether it be from one or two different areas in the chain of transmission].

Mu'ḍal: Such a ḥadīth has two or more than two narrators missing from one area of the chain.

Mu'allaq: In this type of ḥadīth, a narrator is missing from the beginning of the chain.

Mursal: In this ḥadīth, a narrator between the first successor [*tābi'ī*] and the Blessed Prophet ﷺ is missing and the first successor narrates the ḥadīth saying, "The Blessed Prophet ﷺ said...."

THE DEFINITION OF A SAḤĪḤ ḤADĪTH

A ḥadīth is authentic if every narrator in a chain of transmission is of probity [*'adāla*] and thoroughly accurate [*tāmm al-ḍabṭ*]. He must be intelligent, sane, mature and Muslim at the time of narrating the ḥadīth.

Probity means that the narrator is a person of *taqwā* [god-fearing]; he is not a liar and does not commit major sins. If by any chance a major sin is committed, he repents immediately. Such a person also avoids minor sins as much as possible and if he does, he is not consistent upon them. This person avoids transgression [*fisq*] and sexual misconduct [*faḥsh*] of any kind and has a clear sense of honor. He does not commit such acts as are looked upon as disgraceful or disreputable in Islamic society. For example, he will not urinate or eat and drink while standing in public.

A thoroughly accurate person [*al-tāmm al-ḍabṭ*] means that the narrator is extremely intelligent. This person must possess a strong memory so as to preserve the exact wordings of the ḥadīth. It is also important that the words are memorized accurately, leaving no room for doubt about it being authentic.

If the aforementioned criteria are fulfilled by every narrator, from Ṣaḥābī ﵁ to the last narrator, only then will a ḥadīth be authentic. If all the requirements are fulfilled, then the ḥadīth is a sound-in-itself narration [*ṣaḥīḥ li dhātihī*]. If a narrator is lacking in sharpness of memory or is reported to be of bad character but the ḥadīth is corroborated by other aḥādīth, the ḥadīth is a sound narration [*ṣaḥīḥ li ghairihī*].

If the narrator is lacking in some character, which calls for a weakening of the ḥadīth and it is not corroborated by other aḥādīth, it is called a fair narration [*ḥasan*].

If the criteria that makes a ḥadīth authentic or fair is not found in one or more than one narrators, then the ḥadīth is weak. For example, if the narrator does not possess probity or is not thoroughly accurate, and the authenticity of the ḥadīth is affected by it, the ḥadīth will be degraded to a weak ḥadīth.

There are four main branches of ḥadīth. These branches determine how and in what condition the ḥadīth reaches us:

1. **A mass-transmitted ḥadīth [*mutawātir*]**
   A mass-transmitted ḥadīth is a ḥadīth that is transmitted from one generation to the next in such large numbers, that one could not imagine that they conspired to forge it.

2. **A well-known ḥadīth [*mashhūr*]**
   A well-known narration is a ḥadīth in which three people or more narrated a ḥadīth from one generation to the next. This ḥadīth is also called *mustafīḍ*.

3. **A rare ḥadīth [*'azīz*]**
   A rare narration is a ḥadīth in which two people or more narrated a ḥadīth from one generation to the next.

4. **A solitary ḥadīth [*gharīb*]**
   A solitary ḥadīth is a ḥadīth in which only one person narrated a ḥadīth throughout the transmission.

Other terminologies are also used:

5. **An anomalous ḥadīth [*shādh*]**
   A ḥadīth that is authentic, but which conflicts with other aḥādīth that are more authentic than itself.

6. **A preserved ḥadīth [*maḥfūẓ*]**
   A ḥadīth which is authentic, but which conflicts with other aḥādīth that are less authentic than itself.

7. **A declined ḥadīth [*munkar*]**
   A ḥadīth that is weak and which conflicts with other aḥādīth that are authentic.

8. **An accepted ḥadīth [*ma'rūf*]**
   A ḥadīth having a strong narrator and conflicts with a ḥadīth whose narrator is weak.

This is a summary of some of the terminologies used by the ḥadīth masters. A more elaborate glossary and explanation of ḥadīth terminology can be looked up in the works of the ḥadīth masters. However the aforementioned is sufficient enough for one to understand this book and the reality of the ḥadīth. Most of the nomenclature of the ḥadīth masters is jargon for most people, as few will understand it.

DO BUKHĀRĪ AND MUSLIM CONTAIN ALL THE AUTHENTIC AḤADĪTH?

Some people think that a ḥadīth is only authentic if it is in *Bukhārī* and *Muslim*. Some even insist that the whole *dīn* [religion] of Islam is to be found only in *Bukhārī*.

Once, a bedouin came to the Blessed Prophet ﷺ. He accepted Islam and prayed ṣalāt. Once he completed his ṣalāt, he prayed, "O Allah ﷻ, have mercy on me and the Blessed Prophet ﷺ and no one else." His thinking was that, "If I pray for everyone's mercy, the mercy of Allah ﷻ on me will decrease."

The Blessed Prophet ﷺ said to him, "You have confined the vast."[38]

The mercy of Allah ﷻ is vast and so is the knowledge of our dīn. It is absolute ignorance to confine the whole dīn into *Bukhārī*. According to this view, twenty three years of the Blessed Prophet's ﷺ prophethood is limited to the aḥādīth of *Bukhārī*, and everything he every said or did in twenty three years is in *Bukhārī* and nowhere else. It is like saying that "it is too difficult to follow the whole Qur'an; let's just follow the twenty fourth chapter." Now if someone asks about a ruling, this person asks if it is in the twenty-fourth chapter. If he is told, "No, it is in the twenty-first chapter," he says, "Oh, I can't accept that because I only follow the twenty fourth chapter of the Qur'an."

This is the same way some people treat the aḥādīth. If a ḥadīth is in *Bukhārī*, they accept it; but if it is not, it is rejected. All the ḥadīth

---

[38] Ibn Māja, *al-Arḍ Yuṣībuha al-Baul* | Ibn Ḥabbān, *al-Ad'iyya*

masters and scholars are unanimous that there are many authentic aḥādīth besides the aḥādīth of *Bukhārī* and *Muslim.* Even Imam Bukhārī and Imam Muslim never made any such claim.

If anything, they opposed such radical claims. Imam Bukhārī said, "I have only put authentic ḥadīth in my book, but also left many authentic ḥadīth for fear of the book becoming too drawn-out."[39] Imam Muslim writes, "I have not put the whole collection of authentic aḥādīth in my book."[40] This is why Ḥāfiẓ Ibn Ḥajar writes in *Tadrīb al-Rāwī*, "Imam Bukhārī and Imam Muslim did not include all the authentic ḥadīth in their books, nor did they intend to do so."[41]

Not only that, Imam Bukhārī named his book, *al-Jāmi' al-Ṣaḥīḥ al-Musnad al-Mukhtaṣar min Umūr Rasūl Allāh ﷺ wa Ayyāmihī* [*The Authentic and Continuous, Abridged Collection* (of aḥādīth) *from the Blessed Prophet ﷺ and his Days*].

The word *Mukhtaṣar* [abridged] clearly indicates that *Bukhārī* is condensed and does not include the whole gamut of authentic ḥadīth.

IS A ḤADĪTH GIVEN PREFERENCE BECAUSE IT IS IN BUKHĀRĪ OR MUSLIM?

If two ḥadīth conflict with each other and both are being used as evidence for two opposing rulings, then one ḥadīth will not be chosen over the other because one is in *Bukhārī* or *Muslim* and the other not. There must be clear proof for choosing one ḥadīth over another. Ibn Humām writes in *Fatḥ al-Bārī,* "One ḥadīth will

---

[39] Siyar I'lām al-Nubalā, 12/402|Tahdhīb al-Kamāl, 24/442

[40] Muslim, *al-Tashahhud fi al-Ṣalāṭ*

[41] Tadrīb al-Rāwī 1/217

not be preferred over the other because it is a ḥadīth of *Bukhārī.*"[42] What fault is it of the other ḥadīth that Imam Bukhārī didn't include it in his book?

THE SIX BOOKS OF ḤADĪTH AND THE OBJECTIVES OF THE IMAMS

The following six books of aḥādīth are better known as the *al-Ṣiḥāḥ al-Sitta* (the six authentic books of ḥadīth):

1. *Bukhārī*
2. *Muslim*
3. *Abū Dāwūd*
4. *Nisā'ī*
5. *Tirmidhī*
6. *Ibn Māja*

There is no disagreement about the first five books, but the scholars did differ about *Ibn Māja* and as to whether it should be included in the six books of ḥadīth or not. Nonetheless, *Ibn Māja* eventually became famous and established its place amongst the six books of ḥadīth.

Many people think that *al-Ṣiḥāḥ* must mean that the authentic ḥadīth are only found in the six books of ḥadīth, but this assumption is also incorrect. In fact, many of the aḥādīth not admitted in the *al-Ṣiḥāḥ al-Sitta* are equal to, if not stronger than, many of the aḥādīth in the *al-Ṣiḥāḥ al-Sitta*. For example, the aḥādīth of the *Muwaṭṭa'* of Imam Mālik were compiled long before the aḥādīth of *Bukhārī* and it was considered the most authentic book after the book of Allah ﷻ. Even then, Ibn Ḥazam was of the opinion that the *Sharaḥ Ma'ānī al-Āthār* of Imam Ṭaḥāwī was more reliable than the *Muwaṭṭa'* of Imam Mālik.

[42] Fatḥ al-Qadīr, al-Nawāfil, 2/400

The question then remains, if other books contain more authentic aḥādīth than *al-Ṣiḥāḥ al-Sitta*, then why are only the six famous books of aḥādīth called *al-Ṣiḥāḥ al-Sitta*? The truth is that despite their widespread fame and acceptance in the umma, it is still unknown as to how the six books of aḥādīth came to be called *al-Ṣiḥāḥ al-Sitta*.

Ultimately, what matters is that all the authors of these great books put conditions for including a ḥadīth in their books. If those conditions are kept in mind when studying their books, we gain a deeper understanding of the aḥādīth and the knowledge derived from them. For example, we learn the reason behind the authenticity or weakness of aḥādīth or the hidden flaws in the transmission of a ḥadīth. We also learn the correct method of how to deduce rulings from the aḥādīth. This is possibly why they are called *al-Ṣiḥāḥ al-Sitta*.

It is not possible to cover the different fields of ḥadīth in this introduction, but if anyone wishes to learn more, they may always refer back to the many books written on this subject. Here, I will summarize the objectives of each author of the *al-Ṣiḥāḥ al-Sitta* and what they had in mind when compiling aḥādīth for their book.

Bukhārī

Imam Bukhārī's objective was to teach the method of how to deduce rulings from the authentic aḥādīth. Every sub-chapter is given a heading that indicates a ruling deduced from the aḥādīth under that sub-chapter. This is why it is said that the fiqh of Imam Bukhārī is in his headings [*fiqh al-Bukhārī fī Tarajimihī*].

Muslim

Imam Muslim's objective was to compile all the different transmissions of one ḥadīth in one book. For this reason, it is easier to find a specific authentic ḥadīth in *Muslim* than it is in *Bukhārī*.

Nisā'ī

Imam Nisā'ī concentrated on deducing rulings of the Shari'a from the aḥādīth, like Imam Bukhārī. For this reason, the heading of each new sub-chapter is similar to that of a sub-chapter in *Bukhārī*. But Imam Nisā'ī also aimed to compile the aḥādīth that carry hidden flaws in their transmissions. It is his unique style to start a sub-chapter with the aḥādīth that have hidden flaws in their transmission and then analyze them as the ḥadīth masters did. He ends every sub-chapter with the ḥadīth which he considers to be the most authentic in that sub-chapter.

Abū Dāwūd

Imam Abū Dāwūd compiled all the aḥādīth that the jurists bring in support of their rulings; he also includes multiple transmissions of one ḥadīth in his book; also, if a ḥadīth is weak, he will comment on it. However, Imam Abū Dāwūd takes the opposite course of Imam Nisā'ī in that he starts off every sub-chapter with a authentic ḥadīth and ends it with the weakest.

Tirmidhī

Imam Tirmidhī opened new sub-chapters for each ḥadīth or group of ḥadīth used by the jurists. He does not gather multiple transmissions of one ḥadīth like Imam Nisā'ī or Imam Abū Dāwūd. He will usually narrate one ḥadīth that is in favor of one of the four imams in a ruling of the Shari'a under one sub-chapter. Another method employed by Imam Tirmidhī is to narrate the ḥadīth which have never been previously raised by any other of the ḥadīth masters on a specific Shari'a ruling and then indicate to other supporting aḥādīth [on that issue] by saying, "more aḥādīth are narrated on this subject by so and so." This is to show that there are more aḥādīth on the subject. He also frequently quotes the opinions of the jurists on certain issues.

Ibn Māja

Sunan Ibn Māja follows the same pattern as *Sunan Abū Dāwūd* except that the arrangement of aḥādīth in *Sunan Ibn Māja* surpasses *Sunan Abū Dāwūd. Ibn Māja* contains the most number of weak aḥādīth in the *al-Ṣiḥāḥ al-Sitta.*

BRIEF BIOGRAPHIES OF THE GREAT ḤADĪTH MASTERS

In our times, the dearth of Islamic knowledge is so severe that even the imams of our communities are not familiar with the different ḥadīth masters who reigned in the field of aḥādīth, let alone common Muslims. Many self-proclaimed "ḥadīth masters" and others who call themselves the "people of ḥadīth" [*ahl al-ḥadīth*] are completely ignorant of the names of most of the ḥadīth books and the biographies of the great ḥadīth masters who compiled them. Below is a brief introduction to some of the greatest ḥadīth masters.

Imam Bukhārī

He was Muḥammad ibn Ismā'īl and was born in Bukhara on the 13th or 16th of Shawwāl, 194/c810[43] on Friday after 'Aṣr. His father died before he was born. Imam Bukhārī became blind in childhood but his mothers ardent prayers and *du'ās* bore their fruit, and his eyesight was returned. After this, he sought knowledge until the end of his life.

Imam Bukhārī wrote many books including the renowned collection *Ṣaḥīḥ al-Bukhārī*. The original name given to *Ṣaḥīḥ al-Bukhārī* was, *al-Jāmi' al-Ṣaḥīḥ al-Musnad al-Mukhtaṣar min Umūr Rasūl Allāh Ṣalla Allāhu 'alaihi wa Sallam.*

---

[43] The first date is the Hijri date and the second Gregorian. The "c" is an abbreviation of circa.

Ṣaḥīḥ al-Bukhārī is regarded as the most authentic book after the Qur'an, academically and historically. Imam Bukhārī was known to bathe and perform *istikhāra*[44] before recording any ḥadīth into his book. If he felt positively after the *istikhāra*, he admitted the ḥadīth into his book; otherwise, he rejected it. The compilation of *Ṣaḥīḥ al-Bukhārī* was the fruit of sixteen years of meticulous research.

What praise can we bestow on Imam Bukhārī when Allah ﷻ Himself has immortalized his name for past, present and future generations. So without mentioning another word, we lay the subject of his excellence and piety to rest.

Unfortunately, one of the saddest facts in the history of Islam is that the true scholars of Islam and sincere servants of Allah ﷻ always suffered at the hands of their foes. The foes of Imam Bukhārī harassed him until he was forced to pray, "O Allah ﷻ, this earth has become narrow for me despite its vastness. Take me to your abode." Imam Bukhārī died in Samarqand on the eve of *Eid al-Fiṭr* in 256/c870 at the age of sixty two.

Imam Muslim

He was Muslim ibn Ḥajjāj, but was known by his agnomen, Abū al-Ḥasan. Imam Muslim was born in Naishābūr, Iran, in either 204/c820 or 206/c822. Though he authored many books, he is most recognized for his *Ṣaḥīḥ al-Muslim*. It is said that Imam Muslim would never backbite, nor did he speak ill of anyone throughout his life. *Muslim* became so popular amongst the ḥadīth masters that some scholars actually put it above *Bukhārī*; however, most ḥadīth masters rank *Muslim* below *Bukhārī*. It is worth mentioning that the headings of the

[44] A two-unit voluntary ṣalāt in which one seeks guidance from Allah ﷻ in a particular matter.

sub-chapters in *Muslim* are not written by Imam Muslim but by Imam Nawawī.

Imam Muslim died in 261/c875. Many say that the cause of death came after someone once asked him about a ḥadīth. He was so eager to find the ḥadīth that he searched for it immediately after returning home. During his research, he became hungry and kept a basketful of dates next to him. Every little while he picked a date from the basket and continued looking for the ḥadīth. Ultimately, he unknowingly ate so many dates that it became the cause of his death.

Imam Mālik

He was Mālik ibn Anas ibn Mālik ibn Abī 'Āmir and his agnomen was Abū 'Abd Allāh. He was born in 93/c712 in the blessed city of Madina and lived there his entire life. He was honored with the title, "imam of the place of migration." He was exceptional from birth as his mother bore him after carrying him in her womb for three years. His great grandfather was the first in his family to accept Islam. At the time, his great-grandfather lived in Yemen and later migrated to Madina.

Imam Malik's thirst for knowledge began at an early age. His family was so poor that that they were once forced to tear open the ceiling of their house, collect the wooden beams and sell them to survive. However, during that time Imam Mālik vigorously pursued the knowledge of dīn. He was highly intelligent and was gifted with a photographic memory. It is said that once he read something he never forgot it. His love for the Blessed Prophet ﷺ was also exemplary. Once, while he was teaching ḥadīth, a scorpion stung him seventeen times, but he continued teaching and did not move from his spot out of respect for the ḥadīth.

His book was a masterpiece on ḥadīth. Aside from *Musnad Imām Abī Ḥanīfa* [compiled by Imam Abū Ḥanīfa, a contemporary of Imam Mālik], the ḥadīth masters take his book as the cornerstone of all compilations of authentic aḥādīth. He died on the 11th of Rabī' al-Awwal in 179/c795 at the age of eighty-six and was buried in *Jannat al-Baqī'* in Madina.

Imam Tirmidhī

He was Muḥammud ibn 'Īsā and his agnomen was Abū 'Īsā. Born in approximately 209/c825, he was from the city of Tirmidh in Balkh, hence his attribution, Tirmidhī. Imam Tirmidhī was blessed with an outstanding memory and piety. He became blind due to excessive weeping. He was one of the most favored students of Imam Bukhārī, though he was a follower of Imam Shāfi'ī in fiqh and did not accept the rulings of Imam Bukhārī.

In fact, it is amazing that he quotes all the other jurists in his book *Sunan al-Tirmidhī*, but never quotes or even mentions his teacher Imam Bukhārī. After every ḥadīth, Imam Tirmidhī notes the grade of the ḥadīth and then narrates the rulings the imams derive from that ḥadīth. He frequently gave reference to other aḥādīth related to that subject. Regarding his book, Imam Tirmidhī said, "Whosoever has this book in his house has the prophet who speaks in his house."

Imrān ibn 'Allān says, "Imam Bukhārī died leaving no better person behind than Abū 'Īsā in his place in knowledge and piety." Imam Tirmidhī died in 279/c892.

Imam Abū Dāwūd

He was Sulaimān ibn Ash'ath and his agnomen was Abū Dāwūd. Born in 202/c817, he was from the city of Sīstān near the province of Khurāsān. A devoted student of Imam Aḥmad ibn Ḥanbal,

Imam Abū Dāwūd followed the *madhhab* [school] of his teacher. Imam Abū Dāwūd was known for his humility and simplicity.

Imam Abū Ḥātim says, "Imam Abū Dāwūd was the imam of the world in his knowledge, preservation and memorization, understanding, piety and his judiciousness." Allah's ﷻ acceptance of his book is evidenced by its acceptance in the umma. Imam Abū Dāwūd died in 275/c888.

Imam Nisā'ī

His name was Aḥmad ibn Shu'aib ibn 'Alī al-Nisā'ī and his agnomen was Abū 'Abd al-Raḥmān. He was an unsheathed sword against the people of innovation [*bid'a*]. It is said that he fasted every other day throughout his life as Dāwūd عليه السلام did. He followed the madhhab of Imam Shāfi'ī, though others say he followed the madhhab of Imam Aḥmad ibn Ḥanbal. Imam Nisā'ī died in 303/c915.

Imam Ibn Māja

He was Muḥammad ibn Yazīd and his agnomen was Abū 'Abd Allāh. His mother's name was Māja, which is how he came to be known as Ibn Māja. He was born in 209/c824 in Qazwīn, Iran.

All the ḥadīth masters laud the superb organization of the aḥādīth in *Ibn Māja* and also that it is devoid of repetitiveness in aḥādīth. Unlike the other five books of *al-Ṣiḥāḥ al-Ṣitta*, many of the aḥādīth in *Ibn Māja* are exclusive to *Ibn Māja* and cannot be found in any of the other five books.

Imam Aḥmad ibn Ḥanbal

Imam Ahmad ibn Hanbal is famous for his madhhab. His name was Aḥmad ibn Muḥammad ibn Ḥanbal and his agnomen was Abū 'Abd Allāh. Born in Baghdad in 164/c780, he is given the title of "imam of the *Ahl al-Sunna*" [People of the Sunna]. He was pious and austere; one who had nothing to do with the world. He was imprisoned and tortured for challenging the Rationalists [*Mu'tazilas*] [whose doctrine was the official dogma of the 'Abbāsid king at the time] on the doctrine of whether the Qur'an is a creation or not. He persevered and endured the persecutions of the 'Abbāsid king patiently. Through his sacrifices, Allah ﷻ saved the umma from a dangerous threat. His book, *Musnad Aḥmad*, is a fascinating collection of aḥādīth in which he compiled over 40,000 aḥādīth. Imam Aḥmad ibn Ḥanbal passed away in 241/c855.

Imam Dārimī

He was 'Abd Allāh ibn 'Abd al-Raḥmān al-Dārimī and his agnomen was Abū Muḥammad. Born in 181/c797 in Samarqand, Imam Muslim and Imam Nisā'ī were both his students. His book, *Sunan al-Dārimī*, is one of the most important books of ḥadīth. He passed away in 255/c869.

Imam Baihaqī

He was Aḥmad ibn Ḥusain Baihaqī and his agnomen was Abū Bakr. He was born in 384/c994 and authored many great books, the most acclaimed being *Sunan al-Baihaqī.* He followed the Shafi'ī school of fiqh. He died in 456/c1064 in Naishābūr, Iran.

Imam Ibn al-Jauzī

He was 'Abd al-Raḥmān ibn 'Alī and his agnomen was Abū al-Faraj, though he became famous by the name Ibn al-Jauzī. He was born in 517/c1123 in Baghdad. He was a master in many of the different fields of Islamic sciences and was blessed with a penetrating intellect. Amongst his famous works is his collection of fabricated aḥādīth, though he was harsh in his judgment of the aḥādīth. Imam Ibn Jauzī passed away in 597/c1200.

Ibn al-Athīr al-Jazarī

He was born in 544/c1149 on the island of Ibn 'Umar along the bank of the Tigris River. He wrote many books on the subject of aḥādīth. *Al-Nihāya fī Gharīb al-Ḥadīth* is an excellent book in five volumes while the famous, *Jāmi' al-Uṣūl* is a collection of aḥādīth from *Bukhārī*, *Muslim*, *Abū Dāwūd*, *Muwaṭṭa'* and *Nisā'ī* which consists of twelve volumes. Highly favored by the king and his ministers for his decision-making capabilities and for his vast store of knowledge, he was often consulted by them on important matters.

He became paralyzed near the end of his life. The king and his ministers oversaw his treatment, but nothing helped. One man came to him and said, "My treatment always works; you can pay me after you recover." He began treating the shaikh, who indeed began showing signs of recovery.

'Ibn al-Athīr told his brother 'Izz al-Dīn, "Pay this man and send him off."

His brother replied in suprise, "but his treatment is working and you are recovering."

Ibn al-Athīr replied, "This is why I don't want to be treated by him. If I recuperate, I will have to pay visits to the courts of the king and his subjects. Right now, I can at least sit and perform my worship while they come to visit me." After that, his treatment was cut short and he passed away in 606/c1209 at the age of sixty-two.

Ḥāfiẓ ibn Ḥajar

He was Aḥmad ibn 'Alī ibn Muḥammad and his agnomen was Abū al-Faḍl. He is known as Ibn Ḥajar as he was born into the tribe of Ḥajar. He was born on the 22nd of Sha'bān, 773/c1372 in Egypt, though his family was originally from 'Asqalān, a town in Palestine. Orphaned at a young age, after memorization of Qur'an, he studied aḥādīth with Zain al-Dīn 'Irāqī for ten years. In this brief time, he developed a solid foundation in the different fields of aḥadīth.

His commentary of *Bukhārī, Fatḥ al-Bārī,* needs no introduction. His work on aḥādīth was indispensable and for that reason the title ḥāfiẓ became permanently fixed to his name. Eventually, he became known as *ḥāfiẓ al-ḥadīth* in the umma.

He was an avid and fast reader, finishing *Muslim* in two and a half days. Once, he finished the three-volume ḥadīth book, *al-Mu'jam al-Ṣaghīr* between ẓuhr and aṣr. He was a follower of the Shāfi'ī school. He passed away on the 28th of Dhu al-Ḥijja, 852/c1449 in Cairo at the age of seventy-nine.

Mundhirī

His full name was 'Abd al-'Aẓīm ibn 'Abd al-Qawīyy ibn 'Abd Allāh and his agnomen was Abū Muḥammad. His forefathers migrated from Syria, but he was born in 581/c1186 in Egypt. "Nobody could beat Mundhirī in memorization of aḥādīth in his time," wrote Dhahabī.

Mundhirī wrote many books, including the outstanding work *al-Targhīb wa al-Tarhīb.* Though renowned for his piety and integrity, he was most famous for his abstinence. In his book, *al-Targhīb wa al-Tarhīb,* he devoted a whole chapter to the importance of abstinence. He titles the chapter, "*al-Targhīb fi al-Zuhd fi al-Dunyā wa al-Akfā' minhā bi al-Qalīl*" ["Exhortation Towards Abstinence from the Material World and to be Content with Little"].

He compiled 160 aḥādīth under this chapter; no other chapter in the book contained so many aḥādīth. Still unsatisfied, he wrote,

"If we were to write the biographies of the predecessors [*salaf*], we could easily produce a few volumes, but this is not the objective of this book. We wrote this much only for blessing." Mundhirī passed away in 657/c1259 in Egypt.

Abū Dāwūd al-Ṭayālasī

He was Sulaimān ibn Dāwū ibn al-Jārūd al-Ṭayālasī and his agnomen was Abū Dāwūd. He was born in 136/c754. His attribution al-Ṭayālasī comes from the family business of selling shawls [*ṭailasān*]. His forefathers descended from Persia and were sold as slaves in Arabia, but were later freed. Imam Abū Dāwūd al-Ṭayālasī himself was from Basra, Iraq. During those times, Basra and Kufa were centers of learning and so he became learned in the knowledge of dīn from an early age. His sharp memory was a major asset in the study of aḥādīth. A favorite student of the renowned ḥadīth master Shu'ba, Abū Dāwūd al-Ṭayālasī later took his teacher's place. His book, *Sunan Abī Dāwūd al-Ṭayālasī*, is one of the most famous books of ḥadīth. He was a follower of the Ḥanafī madhhab. He passed away in 203/c819 or 204/c820.

Abū Muḥammud Baghawī

He was Ḥusain ibn Mas'ūd ibn Muḥammad al-Farrā' al-Baghawī and his agnomen was Abū Muḥammad. He was born in 433/c1041. People knew him as *Muḥiyy al-Sunna* [Reviver of the Sunnas]. He wrote many books, the most well-known of them, *Sharḥ al-Sunna.* When he wrote *Sharḥ al-Sunna,* the Blessed Prophet ﷺ appeared in his dream and said, "May Allah ﷻ keep you alive the way you revived my Sunna." His other famous book is *Maṣābīḥ al-Sunna*, which is the main text of *Mishkāt al-Maṣābīḥ*. His exegesis of the Qur'an, *Ma'ālim al-Tanzīl* is beautifully written. He was a follower of the Shāfi'ī madhhab. He passed away in 516/c1122.

Jalāl al-Dīn Suyūtī

He was 'Abd al-Raḥmān ibn al-Kamāl Abī Bakr and his agnomen was Abū al-Faḍl. He was born in 849/c1445; his mother died during childbirth. Learned in various disciplines and fields, he authored over six hundred books. He followed the Shafi'ī madhhab. Jalāl al-Dīn Suyūtī passed away in 911/c1505 in Egypt.

Mullā 'Alī Qārī

He was 'Alī ibn Sulṭān Muḥammad al-Qārī and his agnomen was Abū al-Ḥasan. He was born in Herāt, a northern city of Afghanistan. When Sultan Ismā'īl Ṣafawī [a fanatic shiite] sacked Herat and killed the Muslims mercilessly, Mullā 'Alī Qārī migrated to Makka and settled there. He first learned pronunciation [*tajwīd*] of Qur'an and quickly mastered the discipline until he became an expert in recitation of Qur'an. Soon after, he began studying the science of aḥādīth. He wrote many books, including *Mirqāt al-Mafātīḥ*, a brilliant commentary of the ḥadīth book *al-Mishkāt al-Maṣābīḥ,* and reputed to be the best commentary of ḥadīth. Many scholars acknowledge him as the revivalist [*mujaddid*] of the 10th century. He was a follower of the Ḥanafī madhhab. Mullā 'Alī Qārī died in Makka in Shawwal 1114/c1702, and was buried in the main cemetery of Makka, *Jannat al-Mu'allā*.

Abū Ja'far Ṭaḥāwī

His full name was Aḥmad ibn Muḥammad ibn Salama al-Ṭaḥāwī and his agnomen was Abū Ja'far. The name Ṭaḥāwī comes from Taḥā, a small village on the outskirts of Cairo. He was born in 229/c843. Two of his most renowned books are *Sharḥ Ma'ānī al-Āthār* and *Mushkil al-Āthār*. According to Ibn Ḥazm, these two books are more authentic than the *Muwaṭṭa'* of Imam Mālik. Imam Ṭaḥāwī followed the Ḥanafī madhhab. He passed away in 321/c933.

Imam Nawawī

He was Yaḥyā ibn Sharaf al-Nawawī. He was born in Muḥarram, 631/c1233 in Nawa, a small town near Damascus. He showed signs of abstinence early on in life and had little interest in play and games, preferring to spend his time reciting Qur'an. Shaikh Yāsīn said of him, "I saw him when he was ten. Some children urged him to come and play with them, but he ran from them and cried because he wanted to recite the Qur'an." Shaikh Yāsīn later became his spiritual mentor [*murshid*].

Imam Nawawī's father sat him in his shop, but Imam Nawawī occupied all his time there reciting Qur'an. He ate only once during the day and once at night, and spent most of his nights in worship. Many of his books were instant successes and proved to be indispensable assets for the umma. His famous book *Riyādh al-Ṣāliḥīn* was acclaimed for its inspired selection of aḥādīth, and is one of the most widely read books of ḥadīth to this day. Two other books, *Sharḥ al-Muhdhdhab* and *Sharḥ al-Muslim* also were hailed by the umma. A follower of the Shafi'ī madhhab, Imam Nawawī passed away in 676/c1277.

'Abd Allāh ibn Mubārak

His agnomen was Abū 'Abd al-Raḥmān and he was born in 118/c736. His parents were slaves from Turkmenistan who were later freed. He was rich and lived extravagantly, until Allah ﷻ blessed him with guidance. When he came towards dīn, he became the "leader of the believers" [*amīr al-mu'minīn*] of ḥadīth. Imam Bukhārī's teacher Ibn Mahdī once said, "If Ibn Mubārak doesn't know a ḥadīth, we don't know it either." This implies that Ibn

Mubārak had memorized all the aḥādīth and is thus ranked amongst the ḥāfiẓ of ḥadīth. The elderly and pious gathered at his house and derived blessings and benefit from his talks.

Sufyān Thaurī once said, "I wish that one year of my life could be like 'Abd Allāh ibn Mubārak's. I strive to be like him, but I cannot go beyond three days." Once, the king Hārūn al-Rashīd was staying at *al-Riqa* and 'Abd Allāh ibn Mubārak happened to be there also. Crowds of people filled the streets to see 'Abd Allāh ibn Mubārak. One of the King's slave girls came by the balcony of the palace.

"What is going on?" She asked.

"Abd Allāh ibn Mubārak is here," was the reply.

She said, "This is the real kingship; Hārūn al-Rashīd must parade through the streets to fill it with such crowds.

'Abd Allāh ibn Mubārak always sat in the gatherings of Imam Abū Ḥanīfa and prided himself on it. He followed the madhhab of Imam Abū Ḥanīfa. 'Abd Allāh ibn Mubārak died in 181/c797.

Wakī' ibn al-Jarrāḥ

His agnomen was Abū Sufyān and he was born in 129/c746. He was the teacher or teachers' teacher of all the authors of the *al-Ṣiḥāḥ al-Sitta*. A renowned ḥadīth master and jurist, he was also famous for his piety and taqwā, reciting one whole Qur'an every night. Imam Aḥmad ibn Ḥanbal prided himself on being his student. If he ever narrated a ḥadīth from him [Wakī' ibn al-Jarrāḥ] he would say, "I am narrating this ḥadīth from the likes of a person you have never seen in your lives." He was a ardent follower of the Ḥanafī madhhab and lived his life by the rulings of Imam Abū Ḥanīfa. He died in 198/c813.

Yaḥyā ibn Sa'īd l-Qaṭṭān

His agnomen was Abū Sa'īd. He was an expert in the field of the biography of the narrators of ḥadīth. He was the teacher of Imam Aḥmad and 'Alī ibn Madīnī. He recited one Qur'an every night for twenty years and never missed the congregational ṣalāt. His narrations are found in all the six books of ḥadīth. Dhahabī said that Yaḥyā ibn Sa'īd was the first to write on the field of biography of the narrators of ḥadīth. In fiqh, he was a follower of Imam Abū Ḥanīfa. He died in 198/c813 in Basra.

Maḥmūd ibn Aḥmad al-'Ainī

He was Maḥmūd ibn Aḥmad ibn Mūsā al-'Ainī, and his agnomen was Abū Muḥammad. He was born on the 17th of Ramadan, 762/c1361 at a place called 'Ain Tab, which is close to Ḥalb [Aleppo, Syria]. A follower of the Ḥanafī madhhab, he was a scholar of fiqh, ḥadīth and history. Though he wrote many books, he is best known for his commentary of *Bukhārī*, *'Umdat al-Qārī*. This book is highly commended by the scholars. He died on the 4th of Dhu al-Ḥijja, 855/c1451 at the age of ninety three.

Ibn Abī Shaiba

He was 'Abd Allāh ibn Muḥammad ibn Ibrāhīm, and his agnomen was Abū Bakr. He was the teacher of Imam Bukhārī, Muslim, Abū Dāwūd and many other accomplished aḥadīth masters; his narrations can be found in all of their books. His most notable piece of work is the *al-Muṣannaf*, which is distinctive in many ways. It compiles aḥādīth on every Shari'a ruling and incorporates all the narrations of the Ṣaḥāba ﷽. Speaking on Ibn Abī Shaiba's extraordinary memory, Imam Abū Zur'a al-Rāzī once said, "I have not seen a ḥāfiẓ of ḥadīth who equals him." Ibn Abī Shaiba died in 235/c850.